ANNUALS

PERENNIALS

BORDERS

HERBS

THE
JANET BOLTON
COLLECTION

ROSES

HANGING
BASKETS

PRUNING

BULBS

garden notes

ILLUSTRATIONS BY

Janet Bolton

 **A Sterling/Museum Quilts Book**
Sterling Publishing Co., Inc. New York

Published in the USA by Sterling Publishing Company Inc.,
387 Park Avenue South, New York, NY 10016
and by Museum Quilts Publications.
Published in the UK by Museum Quilts (UK) Inc.,
254-258 Goswell Road, London EC1V 7EB
Distributed in Canada by Sterling Publishing
c/o Canadian Manda Group, One Atlantic Avenue, Suite 105
Toronto, Ontario Canada M6K 3E7
Distributed in Australia by Capricorn Link (Australia) Pty Ltd,
P.O. Box 6651, Baulkham Hills, Business Centre,
NSW 2153, Australia

ISBN: 0-8069-3967-2

Printed and bound in Korea

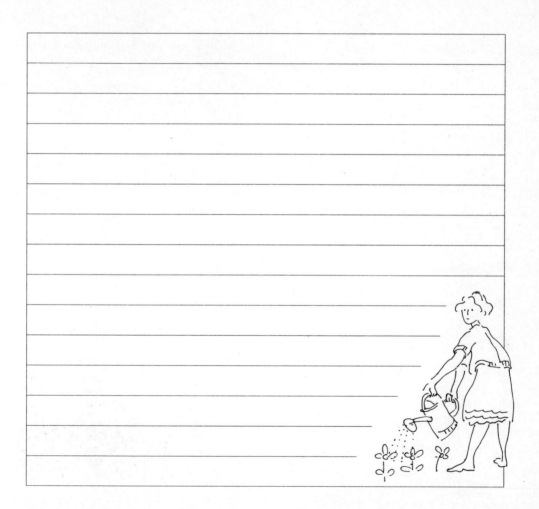

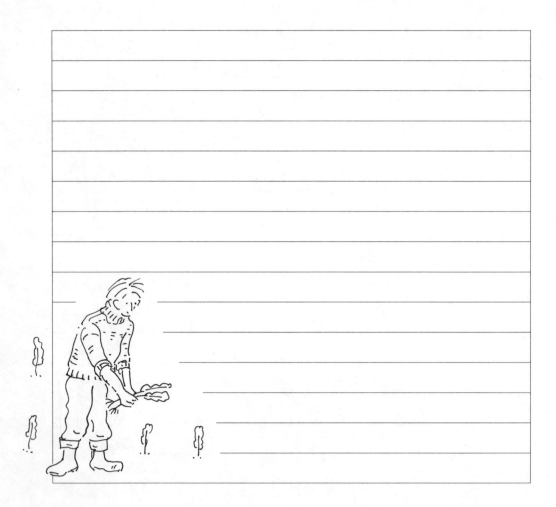

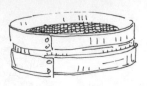

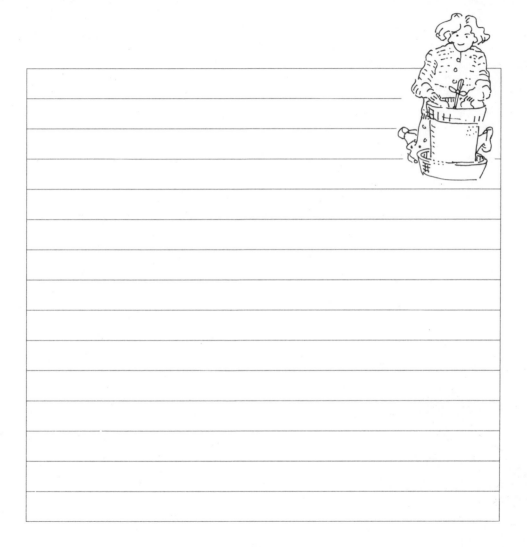

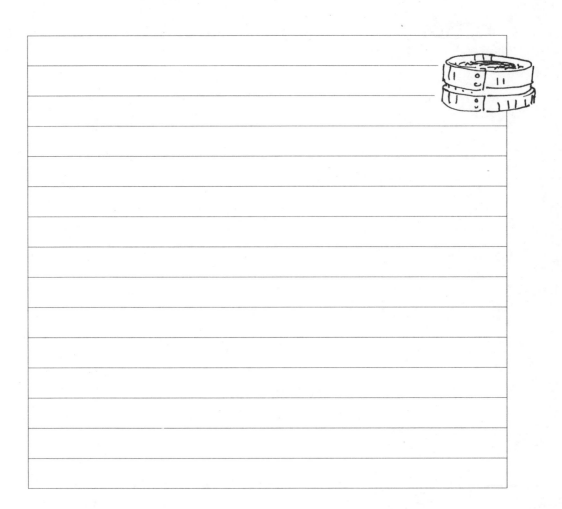